Leighann Lord's
DICT JOKES

Volume One

Why Look It Up When You Can Make It Up!

ALTernate **DEF**initions for Words
You've Probably Never Heard of
But Will Definitely Never Forget

Leighann Lord's
DICT JOKES

Volume One

Why Look It Up When You Can Make It Up!

ALTernate **DEF**initions for Words
You've Probably Never Heard of
But Will Definitely Never Forget

By
Leighann Lord

ISBN: 978-0-9862093-0-7

For my parents who always told me to "look it up." Thank you for that, and more, and everything. You are my favorite Black people.

"If the English language made any sense,
lackadaisical would have something to do
with a shortage of flowers."

Doug Larson

CONTENTS

ACKNOWLEDGEMENTS

While I am grateful to all of my AltDef fans for enjoying my daily word nerdery, I give a very special thanks to Michael Andrews, Joanna Briley, Helene Flur Hinsey, Dana Friedman, and Trish Rudolff. You guys rock! I appreciate your likes and your alt-AltDefs. They are often better than mine and always make me smile. Thanks so much for playing along.

Thanks to all of my English teachers, especially Mrs. Florence McKetney (fifth grade), Sister Ann O'Brien (junior year, high school), and Mrs. H (sophomore year, college). Your passion and commitment annoyed the crap out of me. Thank you for seeing the spark, fanning the flames, and not letting me settle for anything less than my best effort.

Thanks again, of course, to my parents for teaching me the power and beauty of words and for not having a coronary when I changed my major in college from finance to English.

INTRODUCTION

Wouldn't it be easier (and fun) if words meant what they sound like? If:

Canonize meant what spicy food does to your colon?
Faux pas meant fake peace?
Rebuff meant to get undressed?

Well, they do in *THIS BOOK*. I mean, *why look it up when you can make up*, right?

Don't get me wrong. I love words. My mom taught me how to read when I was four years old. I scored reasonably well on the verbal section of the Scholastic Aptitude Test (SAT). I earned my bachelor's degree in journalism and creative writing. One of my favorite songs is Cameo's "Word Up." I date myself to prove a point: I. Love. Words.

But I didn't always.

As a kid, when I came across a word I didn't know my parents told me to look it up. Yeah, I had *those* parents. And by look it up I mean I had to physically get up, haul the Big Ass Dictionary down off the shelf, and search for the word. If for some reason there was no dictionary on hand I was told to figure the word out from the context of the sentence. UG! Sometimes this worked. Sometimes it didn't. What often happened was I defined the word by how it looked or sounded. I was usually wrong, but I almost always liked my **alt**ernate **def**inition better.

HISTRIONICS

(his-tree-ON-iks) noun:
Behavior or speech for effect, as insincere or exaggerated expression of an emotion.

-

The history of Ebonics.

What began as a chore became a skill when I was introduced to Balderdash™. It's a game – think Fictionary meets Scrabble® – where you earn points for picking the actual definition of a word out from amongst the creative ones submitted by fellow players. You also earn points if they pick your fabricated definition. A dubious honor to claim, but I was born for Balderdash™. It was so wrong, but so fun.

I still love coming across new words – which are really old words that have fallen into disuse – and thinking, "This word sounds like it should mean 'this.'"

TORRID

(TOR-id) adjective:
Parched with heat,
especially of the sun; hot.

-

When Tori Spelling is in a bad mood.

I began sharing my alternate definitions
(AltDefs) on social media back in 2011 as
Leighann Lord's Word of the Day (WOTD).

Some are silly...

NUGATORY

(NOO-guh-tor-ee) adjective:
Of little or no consequence; trifling.

-

The factory where caramel
and nougat are made.

... bawdy ....

CICATRIX

(SIK-uh-triks) noun:
New tissue that forms over a wound.

-

A reason why a prostitute considers
quitting the business.

---

and pop culturey:

INSTAURATION

(in-staw-REY-shuhn) noun:
Renewal; restoration; renovation; repair.

-

An Instagram power user.

I was surprised at how much other people
enjoyed my AltDefs. I began getting
comments like:

"I love your word of the day."
"I share this with my students."
"You make me want to read more."
"Hey, I used one of your words today."

People even began asking for my alternate definitions...

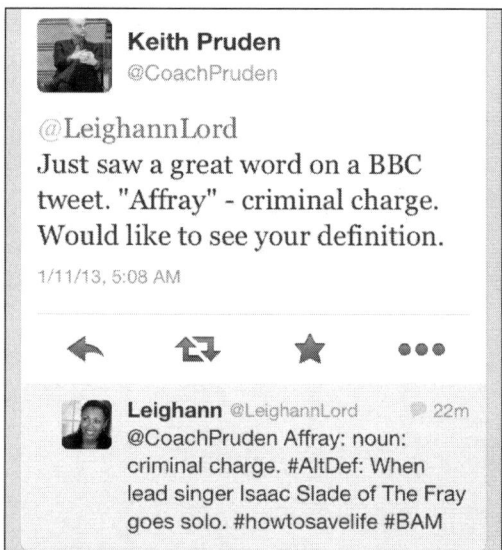

Keith Pruden
@CoachPruden

@LeighannLord
Just saw a great word on a BBC
tweet. "Affray" - criminal charge.
Would like to see your definition.

1/11/13, 5:08 AM

Leighann @LeighannLord 💬 22m
@CoachPruden Affray: noun:
criminal charge. #AltDef: When
lead singer Isaac Slade of The Fray
goes solo. #howtosavelife #BAM

... or to help them find the right word ...

Leighann
@LeighannLord

@NWlady28: Ok, favorite Word lady, is there a word for having a pretend online girlfriend or pathological doping liar? <~ Yes. Thursday.

Since words can have many meanings, fans would send me actual definitions:

VeryFunnyLady.com @Leighan... 4 Sep
#WOTD: jardiniere \jahr-duh-NEER\ n: an ornamental stand for plants or flowers. #ALTDEF: An outstanding marine.

David Grizzly Smith
@Grizzlysgrowls

Jardiniere is also a cooking term: cooksinfo.com/jardiniere Went to cooking school in 1987. :-)
@LeighannLord

The best is when people send me their own
AltDefs:

Leighann Lord
September 17 at 9:01am · Hootsuite · 🌐 ▾

#WOTD: taradiddle \tar-uh-DID-l\ n: Informal. a small lie; fib. #ALTDEF:
Stage directions in season two of "True Blood."

Like · Comment · Share

👍 Christina Soto, Joy Steele, Chris Griggs and 5 others like this.

Ayanna Rolette Lol!!
September 17 at 9:07am · Like

Michael Andrews #AltDef2: When a tarantula tap dances with Ben Vereen.
September 17 at 9:29am · Like · 👍 2

Helene Fluhr Hinsey Alt Def#3: A little hanky-panky on the grounds of
Scarlet's ancestral home (See "Gone with the Wind").
September 17 at 11:36am · Unlike · 👍 4

Dana Friedman AltDef #4: A rip-roaring beginning to a drum solo. (In case
that's too obscure, FF to :20 : https://www.youtube.com/watch?v=Dst0AdVB21Q
)

▶ **Drum Rudiments #16 - Single Paradiddle -
DrumRudiments.com**
An instructional drum lessons video demonstrating one of...
YOUTUBE.COM

13 hrs · Unlike · 👍 1 · Remove Preview

Leighann Lord Dana, This tickles me because I was a drummer in my high
school marching band and paradiddles were one of the first things we learned.
Just now · Like

My inner teacher and outer comedian have come to think of my AltDefs as Dict (short for "dictionary") Jokes. I share them to enlighten and entertain. You might also experience:

An increased vocabulary;
A desire to retake the SAT:
Remembering an AltDef instead of the actual definition;
Using a word incorrectly;
Using a word correctly;
An urge to look up new words on your smart phone's dictionary app (Yes, you do have one. It's probably in the utilities folder.)
And best of all you might remember a Dict Joke and start giggling to yourself for no apparent reason at an inappropriate time.

Dict Jokes are best, of course, when shared so after some not-so-subtle hints from fans I have compiled my alternate definitions into a book. Welcome. Enjoy. Share.

THE FORMAT

THE WORD
(Pronunciation) Part of speech
(noun, verb, adjective, adverb, etc.):
Definition.

-

My alternate definition.

A

ABEYANCE

(uh-BAY-unss) noun:
Temporary inactivity;
suspension.

-

Doing what Beyoncé says.

ABJURE

(ab-JOOR) verb:

To renounce upon oath.

-

A legal workout.

ABNEGATE

(AB-nih-gayt) verb:

Deny, renounce.

-

The magic word you say

to open a closed gate.

ABSTERGENT

(ab-STUR-juhnt) adjective:

1. Cleansing. 2. Purgative.

-

To refrain from doing laundry.

ACCOUTREMENT

(uh-KOO-ter-munt) noun:
Equipment, trappings;
specifically: a soldier's outfit
usually not including
clothes and weapons.

-

A French accountant.

ACME

(AK-mee) noun:

The highest point of something;

the highest level

or degree attainable.

-

Coyote arms supplier.

AD REM

(ad REM) adverb:
Without digressing; in a
straightforward manner.

-

When your dreams have
commercials in them.

ADAMANTINE

(ad-uh-MAN-teen) adjective:
Utterly unyielding
or firm in attitude.

-

A Valentine's Day card
from Wolverine.

ADROIT

(uh-DROIT) adjective:
Cleverly skillful, resourceful,
or ingenious.

-

A transgender android.

ADULATE

(AJ-uh-layt) transitive verb:
To flatter or admire slavishly.

-

When a judge renders a verdict
after business hours.

AGNOMEN

(ag-NOH-muhn) noun:

A nickname.

-

An upset stomach.

AGON

(AH-gahn) noun:
Conflict; especially the
dramatic conflict between
the chief characters
in a literary work.

-

When a Caribbean man
leaves you. "He agon."

ALEMBIC

(uh-LEM-bik) noun:
Anything that transforms,
purifies, or refines.

-

Alec Baldwin and Glen Beck's
Hollywood couple name.

ANTIPODE

(AN-ti-pohd) noun:

A direct or exact opposite.

-

An enemy or adversary

of Edgar Allan Poe.

APOLLONIAN

(ap-uh-LOH-nee-uhn) adjective:

Serene; harmonious;

disciplined; well-balanced.

-

A member of Apollonia 6.

ARBALEST

(AHR-buh-list) noun:

A crossbow especially

of medieval times.

-

A tree molester.

ARGOSY

(AHR-GUH-see) noun:

A rich source or supply.

-

When a pirate tells you
to go check something out.

ARMAMENTARIUM

(ahr-muh-muhn-TAIR-ee-uhm)

noun:

A fruitful source of devices or
materials available or used
for an undertaking.

-

A weapons museum.

ASSAY

(a-SEY) verb:

To examine or analyze.

-

How Foghorn Leghorn

starts every sentence.

AUREATE

(AWR-ee-it) adjective:
Characterized by an ornate
style of writing or speaking.

-

Sounding like an idiot.

AUSCULTATION

(aw-skuhl-TEY-shuhn) noun:
The act of listening to sounds
within the body
as a method of diagnosis.

-

Ass worship.

50

AUTOLOGOUS

(ah-TOL-uh-guhs) adjective:
Involving a situation in which
the donor and the recipient
(of blood, skin, bone, etc.)
are the same person.

-

IRS car log.

B

BACCATE

(BAK-eyt) adjective:
Berrylike.

-

What you play on a
discount golf course.

BACCHANAL

(BAK-uh-nal, -nahl) noun:

A wild and drunken celebration.

-

Opposite of the front canal.

BANAUSIC

(buh-NAW-sik) adjective:
Serving utilitarian purposes
only; mechanical; practical.

Burned plantains.

BANDERSNATCH

(BAN-der-snach) noun:
An imaginary wild animal
of fierce disposition.

-

A cover band.

BANDY

(BAN-dee) verb:

To pass from one to another

or back and forth;

give and take.

-

A band where no one plays

an actual instrument.

BATHETIC

(buh-THET-ik) adjective:
Displaying or characterized by
insincere emotions.

-

Drowning in the bathtub.

BEDIZEN

(bih-DYE-zun) verb:

To dress or adorn gaudily.

-

Falling asleep while meditating.

BEGRUDGE

(bi-GRUHJ) transitive verb:

To envy or resent

someone's good fortune.

-

To be at peace with

your inner pettiness.

BELLETRISTIC

(bel-li-TRIS-tik) adjective:
Related to literature regarded
as a fine art, especially as
having a purely aesthetic
function.

-

Behavior characteristic of
Bellatrix Lestrange.

BIDDABLE

(BID-uh-bul) adjective:
Easily led, taught,
or controlled; docile.

-

Getting a good hand in spades,
bridge, or bid whist.

BIDENTATE

(by-DEN-tayt) adjective:
Having two teeth
or toothlike parts.

-

Joe Biden's tenure as Vice
President of the United States.

BILDUNGSROMAN

(BIL-doongz-roh-mahn) noun:
A type of novel concerned with
the education, development,
and maturing of a young
protagonist.

-

A fusion of Dutch
and Roman architecture.

BILLET-DOUX

(bil-ay-DOO) noun:

A love letter.

-

When a couple lives together
to share expenses.

BLEB

(bleb) noun:

A bubble.

-

The sound your lips make when
you strum them with your
finger.

BORBORYGMUS

(bor-buh-RIG-mus) noun:
Intestinal rumbling
caused by moving gas.

-

The love child of Ernest
Borgnine and Don Imus.

BRUIT

(BROOT) verb:

Report, rumor.

-

How you make
beer and coffee.

C

CACOLOGY

(ka-KOL-uh-jee) noun:
Defectively produced speech;
socially unacceptable diction.

-

The study of excrement.

CAHOOT

(kuh-HOOT) noun:
Partnership, league —
usually used in plural.

-

An owl from California.

CALLIPYGOUS

(kal-uh-PY-guhs) adjective:
Having well-shaped buttocks.

-

The disease you can sometimes
get from over-using said
buttocks.

CANONIZE

(KAN-uh-nahyz) verb:
To glorify and honor.

-

What spicy food
can do to your colon.

CATAWAMPUS

(kat-uh-WOM-puhs) adjective:

Askew; awry;

positioned diagonally.

-

A cat fight.

CATECHIZE

(KAT-i-kahyz) verb:

To question closely.

-

Cat circumcision.

CATHOLICON

(kuh-THOL-i-kuhn) noun:

A universal remedy; panacea.

-

ComicCon for Catholics.

CHAPTALIZE

(SHAP-tuh-lahyz) verb:
To increase the alcohol
in a wine by adding sugar.

-

To put on ChapStick.

CHOP-CHOP

(chop-chop) adverb:
Quickly.

-

What scissor-happy
hairdressers do.

CICATRIX

(SIK-uh-triks) noun:
New tissue that
forms over a wound.

-

A reason why a prostitute
considers quitting
the business.

CIMMERIAN

(si-MEER-ee-uhn) adjective:

Very dark; gloomy; deep.

-

The name of a sci-fi villain

or a late 20th-century

urban child.

CLIMACTERIC

(kly-MAK-tuh-rik) noun:
1. A major turning point or
critical stage; 2. Menopause.

-

Female climate change.

COGNOSCENTE

(kahn-yuh-SHEN-tee) noun:
A person who has expert
knowledge in a subject;
connoisseur.

-

A smart cog in the wheel.

COMIX

(KAH-miks) noun:

Comic books or comic strips.

-

The various forms of

communism.

COMMEMORATE

(kuh-MEM-uh-rayt) verb:
To call to remembrance.

-

Back when your savings
account earned interest.

COMPLICE

(KOM-plis) noun:

An associate; accomplice.

-

Free range lice.

CONCATENATE

(kon-KAT-n-eyt) verb:

To link together;

unite in a series or chain.

-

A large gathering of cats.

CONNIPTION

(kuh-NIP-shuhn) noun:

A fit of hysterical

excitement or anger.

-

How old Black women express

their deep displeasure.

CONSUETUDINARY

(kon-swi-TOOD-n-er-ee)

adjective:

Customary.

-

When a Latin woman

has an attitude.

CONVERSAZIONE

(kahn-ver-saht-see-OH-nee)

noun:

A meeting for conversation
especially about art,
literature, or science.

-

How Italian gangsters
talk to each other.

COPIOUS

(KOH-pee-us) adjective:

Yielding something abundantly.

-

When women go

to the bathroom

in groups of two or more.

CORPUS DELICTI

(KOR-puhs di-LIK-ty) noun:
The concrete evidence that
shows that a crime has been
committed.

-

Someone who enjoys
necrophilia and cannibalism.

CRASIS

(KREY-sis) noun:
Composition; constitution;
makeup.

-

How Australians say
the word "crisis."

CRITIQUE

(kruh-TEEK) noun:
An act of criticizing; especially
a critical estimate or
discussion.

-

One of the X-Men;
Mystique's mother.

CUNCTATOR

(kungk-TAY-tuhr) noun:
One who hesitates; a
procrastinator or delayer.

-

One who enjoys watching *Real
Housewives*
reality TV shows.

D

DE MINIMIS

(dee-MIN-uh-mus) adjective:
Lacking significance or
importance; so minor as
to merit disregard.

-

Mini-Me's progeny.

DEADPAN

(DED-pan) adjective:
Marked by or accomplished
with a careful pretense of
seriousness or calm
detachment.

-

A murder weapon.

DEFENESTRATION

(dee-fen-uh-STREY-shun) noun:
A throwing of a person or thing
out of a window.

-

An arms buildup.

DERRING-DO

(dair-ing-DOO) noun:

Daring action; daring.

-

Going to the bathroom in an

unfamiliar place.

DESIDERATUM

(dih-sid-uh-RAH-tum) noun:

Something desired

as essential.

-

Ditching your date in the

desert.

DEUCEDLY

(DOO-sid-lee) adverb:

Devilishly; damnably.

-

Stewie-Griffin style.

DEVOIR

(duh-VWAHR) noun:
Duty, responsibility.

-

French fast food.

DILETTANTE

(DIL-i-tahnt, dil-i-TAHNT) noun:
One who takes up an activity
or interest in a superficial way.

-

A pickle-loving debutante.

DIONYSIAN

(dy-uh-NIS-ee-uhn) adjective:
Uninhibited; undisciplined;
spontaneous; wild; orgiastic.

-

The God of death.

DIPLOPIA

(dih-PLOH-pee-uh) noun:
Double vision.

-

When excrement hits the toilet
bowl water forcefully enough to
cause splash back.

DISAPPROBATION

(dis-ap-ruh-BAY-shun) noun:
The act or state of disapproving.

-

Committing a crime
while on probation.

DISHABILLE

(dis-uh-BEEL) noun:
The state of being
partly dressed.

-

Gossiping about
Jennifer Beals.

DIVERTISSEMENT

(dih-VER-tiss-munt) noun:

A dance sequence or

short ballet usually

used as an interlude.

-

False advertising.

DOWAGER

(DOU-uh-jer) noun:
An elderly woman of
stately dignity, especially
one of elevated social position.

-

Betting on the deer
instead of the hunter.

DOYENNE

(doi-EN) noun:
A woman who is the senior
member of a group, class,
or profession.

-

The back half of a
Wendy Williams greeting.

DRAGGLE

(DRAG-uhl) verb:

To soil by dragging over

damp ground or in mud.

-

Slow motion drag racing.

DUOPSONY

(doo-OP-suh-nee) noun:
A market condition in which
there are only two buyers, thus
exerting great influence on
price.

-

The study of Doo Wop.

DYSTHYMIA

(dis-THY-mee-uh) noun:

A mild depression.

-

Pulling a muscle in your thigh.

E

ELIXIR

(ih-LIK-ser) noun:
A medicinal concoction.

-

How British men
give oral sex.

EMULOUS

(EM-yuh-luhs) adjective:
Eager to imitate, equal,
or to surpass another.

-

A lost emu.

ENSCONCE

(en-SKONS) verb:

To settle securely or snugly.

-

To dive face first into

a plate of scones.

EPITHET

(EP-uh-thet) noun:
A bad, disparaging or
abusive word or phrase.

-

How Boba Fett
handles his allergies.

EPITOME

(ih-PIT-uh-mee) noun:

A summary of a written work.

-

A sympathy email.

ESCULENT

(ES-kyuh-luhnt) noun:

Something edible,

especially a vegetable.

-

Giving up Lent for Lent.

EUDEMONIA

(yoo-di-MOH-nee-uh) noun:

Happiness; well-being.

-

The first person in the house

to get pneumonia.

EX OFFICIO

(EKS uh-FISH-ee-oh) adjective:

By virtue of one's

official position.

-

When the divorce is final.

EXEGESIS

(ek-suh-JEE-sis) noun:
Exposition, explanation;
especially an explanation or
critical interpretation of a text.

-

Stage directions in
Jesus Christ Superstar.

EXIGENT

(EK-suh-junt) adjective:
Requiring immediate
aid or action.

-

What a man does when
a woman asks him to leave.

EXTEMPORIZE

(ik-STEMP-puh-ryze) verb:

Improvise.

-

When a temp becomes

a full-time employee.

F

FABULIST

(FAB-yuh-list) noun:

1. A liar. 2. A person who invents

or relates fables.

-

The Ford Modeling

Agency roster.

FANTAST

(FAN-tast) noun:

A visionary or dreamer.

-

When you're too busy to say

the word "fantastic."

FARD

(fahrd) verb:

To apply cosmetics.

-

Difficulty passing gas.

FAUX PAS

(fo PAH) noun:
A blunder, especially
a social mistake.

-

Fake peace.

FELICITATE

(fih-LISS-uh-tayt) verb:

To consider happy or fortunate.

-

To pontificate about

the TV show *Felicity*.

FILIOPIETISTIC

(fil-ee-oh-pahy-i-TIS-tik)

adjective:

Pertaining to reverence of

forebears or tradition,

especially if carried to excess.

-

The love of pie.

FLAGITIOUS

(fluh-JISH-uhs) adjective:
Extremely wicked or criminal.

-

A flatulent rapper.

FLANEUR

(flah-NUHR) noun:

An idler or loafer;

a man about town.

-

A fancy flannel nightgown.

FOOL'S PARADISE

(foolz PAR-uh-dys) noun:

A state of happiness

based on false hopes.

-

The American Dream.

FORTE

(fort, FOHR-tay) noun:
A strong point; something in
which a person excels.

-

The average age
of a mid-life crisis.

FOUR-FLUSH

(FOR-FLUSH) verb:
To bluff in poker holding
a four flush.

-

A sign it's time
to call a plumber.

FRACAS

(FREY-kuhs) noun:

A noisy, disorderly disturbance

or fight; riotous brawl; uproar.

-

An orgy on

Battlestar Galactica.

FROLIC

(FRAH-lik) verb:

To amuse oneself;

make merry.

-

Finger-licking good broccoli.

FUGACIOUS

(fyoo-GAY-shus) adjective:

Lasting a short time;

evanescent.

-

Cute but forgettable.

FURLONG

(FER-lawng) noun:

A unit of distance equal to 220
yards (about 201 meters).

-

A full-length mink coat.

FUSTIAN

(FUSS-chin) noun:

A strong cotton
and linen fabric.

-

A fussy person.

G

GAMP

(gamp) noun:

A large umbrella.

-

An elderly scamp.

GARNITURE

(GAHR-nih-cher) noun:
Embellishment, trimming.

-

Red furniture.

GASCON

(GAS-kuhn) noun:

A braggart.

adjective: Boastful.

-

The guy you holler at
to give you more wine when
you've already had too much.

GASSER

(GAS-er) noun:

Something that is

extraordinarily pleasing.

-

When a man expels gas

in the presence of a woman.

GERMINAL

(JUR-muh-nl) adjective:
Being in the earliest stage
of development.

-

A dirty urinal.

GLOM

(glom) verb:

To latch onto something.

-

Faded glamour.

GLOZE

(glohz) verb:

To minimize or to

explain away.

-

Lip gloss made from Vaseline

and Kool-Aid mix.

GORGONIZE

(GOR-guh-nyze) verb:
To have a paralyzing or
mesmerizing effect on;
stupefy, petrify.

-

Eating too much cheese.

GRADGRIND

(GRAD-grynd) noun:
Someone who is solely
interested in cold, hard facts.

-

Working toward your
masters or PhD.

GROUSE

(grous) verb:

To grumble; complain.

-

A green house.

H

HAIMISH

(HEY-mish) adjective:
Homey; cozy and
unpretentious.

-

The District 12 winner
of the *Hunger Games*
before Katniss and Peeta.

HALCYON

(HAL-see-un) adjective:

Calm, peaceful.

-

Watching *2001: A Space Odyssey* and *Battlestar Galactica* back to back.

HEADLONG

(HED-LAWNG) adverb:

With the head foremost.

-

The result of using forceps.

HEBEPHRENIA

(hee-buh-FREE-nee-uh) noun:
A form of insanity occurring
at puberty, also known as
disorganized schizophrenia.

-

Crazy about marijuana.

HIATUS

(hye-AY-tus) noun:

A break in or as if

in a material object; gap.

-

TV show purgatory.

HIBERNIAN

(hy-BUR-nee-uhn) adjective:
Of or relating to Ireland.

-

Someone who hibernates.

HIRCINE

(HUR-sahyn) adjective:
Of, pertaining to,
or resembling a goat.

-

A sane woman.

HISTRIONICS

(his-tree-ON-iks) noun:
Behavior or speech for effect, as
insincere or exaggerated
expression of an emotion.

-

The history of Ebonics.

HSIEN

(shyuhn) noun:
One of a group of
benevolent spirits promoting
good in the world.

-

A wallflower.

HYDROMANCY

(HYE-druh-man-see) noun:
Divination by the appearance or
motion of liquids (as water).

-

The secret life of fire hydrants.

HYPOTHECATE

(hye-PAH-thuh-kayt) verb:
To make an assumption for the
sake of argument.

-

Injecting your cat with
medicine.

I

INCOGNITO

(in-kog-NEE-toh) adverb,
adjective:
Having one's identity
concealed.

-

When Magneto is
wearing street clothes.

INCOMMODIOUS

(in-kuh-MOH-dee-uhs) adjective:
Inconvenient or uncomfortable.

-

Bathroom meetings.

INTEGUMENT

(in-TEG-yuh-muhnt) noun:

1. A natural covering,
as a skin, shell, or rind.
2. Any covering, coating,
enclosure, etc.

-

Long-lasting chewing gum.

INTERCALATE

(in-TER-kuh-layt) verb:
To insert (as a day) in a
calendar.

-

The formula to figure out
which minority culture
arrives the latest.

INTERPOLATION

(in-tur-puh-LEY-shuhn) noun:
The act or process of
introducing something
additional or extraneous
between other parts.

-

Interpretive pole dancing.

INWIT

(IN-wit) noun:

1. Conscience.

2. Reason, intellect.

3. Courage.

-

Being on the inside

of an inside joke.

IRRIGUOUS

(ih-RIG-yoo-uhs) adjective:

Well-watered, as land.

-

Irregular bowel movements.

INSTAURATION

(in-staw-REY-shuhn) noun:

Renewal; restoration;

renovation; repair.

-

An Instagram power user.

J

JOINTURE

(join-cher) noun:

Property given to a woman

upon marriage, to be owned by

her

after her husband's death.

-

The aches and pains

of old age.

JUBILEE

(JOO-bih-lee) noun:

A special anniversary of an
event, especially a 50th
anniversary.

-

A Jewish person
who lives in the Deep South.

JUNKET

(JUNK-ut) noun:

A promotional trip made at
another's expense.

-

What you do with an old car.

JUNOESQUE

(joo-noh-ESK) adjective:
Having a stately bearing and
regal beauty; statuesque.

-

When a pregnant teenager
begins showing.

185

K

KICKSHAW

(KIK-shaw) noun:

1. A fancy dish; delicacy.

2. A trinket.

-

A rickshaw pulled by a Radio
City Music Hall Rockette.

KITSCH

(KITCH) noun:

A tacky or lowbrow quality

or condition.

-

A small kitchen.

KOWTOW

(KOU-TOU) verb:

To act in an obsequious manner;
show servile deference.

-

When a cow breaks down and
needs to be moved.

L

LARRUP

(LAR-uhp) verb:

To beat or thrash.

-

When laryngitis has

run its course.

LENTICULAR

(len-TIK-yuh-ler) adjective:
Having the shape of
a double-convex lens.

-

Being very particular about
what you give up for Lent.

LEVIGATE

(LEV-i-geyt) verb:
To rub, grind, or
reduce to a fine powder.

-

A blue jeans scandal.

LIEGE

(leej, leezh) noun:

1. A feudal lord.

2. A vassal or subject.

-

A lesion that's just about
healed.

LISSOTRICHOUS

(li-SO-tri-kuhs) adjective:
Having straight or smooth hair.

-

The purpose of lying.

LITTORAL

(LIT-er-uhl) adjective:
Pertaining to the shore of
a lake, sea, or ocean.

-

The goal of 100% global
literacy.

LOGOMACHY

(luh-GOM-uh-kee) noun:

1. A dispute about words.

2. A battle fought with words.

-

The science of creating logos.

LUNETTE

(loo-NET) noun:

Something that has the shape

of a crescent or half-moon.

-

A mentally unstable brunette.

M

MACARONIC

(mak-uh-RON-ik) adjective:
Composed of a mixture
of languages.

-

How you look
doing the Macarena.

MAKEBATE

(MEYK-beyt) noun:

A person who causes

contention or discord.

-

When an underage girl dresses

like a grown woman.

MALADROIT

(mal-uh-DROYT) adjective:
Lacking skill, cleverness,
or resourcefulness
in handling situations.

-

An android with
a bad attitude.

MALEDICTION

(mal-uh-DIK-shun) noun:

A curse.

-

A negative sexual experience.

MALVERSATION

(mal-ver-SAY-shun) noun:

Misconduct in public office.

-

Speaking ill of the dead.

MAMMONISM

(MAM-uh-niz-uhm) noun:
The greedy pursuit of riches.

-

The practice of calling
a woman "ma'am."

MANIFOLD

(MAN-uh-fohld) adjective:

Of many kinds;

numerous and varied.

-

When a man does laundry.

MATRILINEAL

(ma-truh-LIN-ee-uhl) adjective:
Inheriting or determining
descent through the female line.

-

Laying a mattress
perpendicular to the box spring.

MENTOR

(MEN-tohr, -tuhr) noun:
A wise and trusted
counselor or teacher.

-

Someone who shares
their Mentos.

MEWL

(myool) verb:

To cry, as a baby; whimper.

-

An unattractive shoe choice

for thin-legged women.

MICAWBER

(mih-KAW-buhr) noun:

An eternal optimist.

-

A bird whose call sounds
like Mick Jagger.

MIGNON

(min-YON) adjective:

Small and pretty.

-

A 60-second yawn.

MOIETY

(MOY-uh-tee) adjective:
One of two equal parts; half.

-

How Moët tastes.

MONOLOGY

(muh-NOL-uh-jee) noun:

A long speech by someone.

-

The study of *Monopoly*.

MUGWUMP

(MUHG-wuhmp) noun:
A person who is neutral
or uncommitted,
especially in politics.

-

Beating up muggles.

MULTITUDINOUS

(mul-tuh-TOO-duh-nus)

adjective:

Including a multitude of
individuals.

-

Cranky multiple personalities.

N

NARY

(NAIR-ee) adjective:
Not any; no; never a.

-

Using too much Nair
to shave your legs.

NEOTERISM

(nee-OT-uh-riz-uhm) noun:

An innovation in language,
as a new word, term,
or expression.

-

Terrorist best practices.

NOCTILUCENT

(nok-tuh-LOO-suhnt) adjective:
Visible during the short
night of the summer.

-

Beautiful by moonlight.

NOOSPHERE

(NOH-uh-sfeer) noun:
The sum of human knowledge,
thought, and culture.

-

The fear of being lynched.

NOTORIOUS

(noh-TOR-ee-us) adjective:
Generally known and talked of;
especially widely
and unfavorably known.

-

A dead rapper set to make
a 3D holographic comeback.

NOVATION

(noh-VEY-shuhn) noun:
The introduction of something
new; innovation.

-

When an audience walks out
on a bad performance.

NUANCE

(NOO-ahnss) noun:
A subtle distinction

or variation.

-

A first-time aunt.

NUGATORY

(NOO-guh-tor-ee) adjective:
Of little or no consequence;
trifling.

-

The factory where caramel and
nougat are made.

NUMEN

(NOO-min) noun:
Divine power, especially one
who inhabits a particular
object.

-

Jerry Seinfeld's mortal enemy.

O

OFTENTIMES

(AW-fun-tymez) adverb:

Often, repeatedly.

-

When a hitman is on the job.

ONIOMANIA

(oh-nee-uh-MEY-nee-uh) noun:
Compulsive shopping;
excessive, uncontrollable desire
to buy things.

-

A love of onions.

ORACULAR

(aw-RAK-yuh-ler) adjective:

Ambiguous; obscure.

-

Buying off the back of the truck

vs. off the rack.

ORECTIC

(aw-REK-tik) adjective:
Of or pertaining to desire;
appetitive.

-

Someone who gives up
their Oreck vacuum cleaner
for a Dyson.

ORTHOSIS

(awr-THOH-sis) noun:

Correction of neurotic state.

-

When your feet smell.

OUTRANCE

(oo-TRAHNS) noun:

The utmost extremity.

-

Playing *Trans-Europe Express*
on a loop on your iPod.

OVERSLAUGH

(OH-ver-slaw) verb:
To pass over or disregard
by giving a promotion
to another instead.

-

When you're tired
of eating cold slaw.

P

PACE

(PAY-see) preposition:
Contrary to the opinion of;
usually used as an expression
of deference to someone's
contrary opinion.

-

Pay first; see later.

PACHYDERM

(PAK-i-durm) noun:

An elephant.

-

The rough skin that develops

on the shoulder you carry

your backpack on.

PACIFY

(PASS-uh-fye) verb:
To allay the anger
or agitation of; soothe.

-

Forgetting your WI-FI
password.

PALADIN

(PAL-uh-din) noun:

A heroic champion.

—

A low noise.

PALLADIUM

(puh-LAY-dee-uhm) noun:

1. A safeguard.

2. A rare, silvery-white metal.

-

A classic NYC nightclub.

PALTER

(PAWL-ter) verb:

1. To talk or act insincerely or deceitfully; lie or use trickery.

2. To bargain with; haggle.

-

A purple halter.

PANDECT

(PAN-dekt) noun:

A complete code of the laws
of a country or system of law.

-

A well-dressed panda.

PARAGON

(PAR-uh-gohn) noun:
A model of excellence
or perfection.

-

When a neophyte
sorority sister
"borrows" your paraphernalia.

PAREGMENON

(puh-REG-muh-non) noun:
The juxtaposition of words
that have a common derivation,
as in "sense and sensibility."

-

AA for paralegals.

PARONYMOUS

(puh-RON-uh-muhs) adjective:
Containing the same root or
stem, as the words
"wise" and "wisdom."

-

Love of piranha.

PERDURE

(puhr-DOOR, -DYOOR)

intransitive verb:

To continue to exist; endure.

-

Free-range chicken that
comes from a good family.

PERSNICKETY

(per-SNIK-i-tee) adjective:

Overparticular; fussy.

-

Getting paid in Snickers bars.

PERSPICACIOUS

(pur-spi-KEY-shuhs) adjective:
Having keen mental perception
and understanding; discerning.

-

A big, roomy handbag.

PETTIFOG

(PET-ee-fog) verb:

To bicker or quibble over trifles

or unimportant matters.

-

Briefly distracted or caught up

in your own thoughts.

PHANTASM

(FAN-taz-um) noun:

A product of fantasy.

-

A very scary horror movie.

PICEOUS

(PIS-ee-uhs) adjective:

Inflammable; combustible.

-

The Greek God of Urine.

PIQUANT

(PEE-kunt) adjective:
Agreeably stimulating
to the palate.

-

Difficulty urinating.

PLENUM

(PLEE-nuhm) noun:

A full assembly, as a joint

legislative assembly.

-

To beg until the other

person gives in.

POCHISMO

(poh-CHEEZ-moh) noun:
An English word or expression
borrowed into Spanish.

-

When a man thinks
his beer gut is sexy.

POCOCURANTE

(poh-koh-koo-RAN-tee) noun:
Caring little; indifferent;
nonchalant.

-

Kinda hot.

PREANTEPENULTIMATE

(pri-an-tee-pi-NUHL-tuh-mit)

adjective:

Fourth from the last.

-

Put up or shut up.

PREDIAL

(PREE-dee-uhl) adjective:

Of or relating to land,

farming, etc.

-

Before showering.

PROPINQUITY

(pruh-PING-kwuh-tee) noun:

Nearness of blood; kinship.

-

The ability to be

proper and witty.

PYROTECHNICS

(pye-ruh-TEK-niks) noun:

A display of fireworks.

-

A group of arsonist

computer geeks.

Q

QUIETUS

(kwye-EE-tus) noun:

Final settlement

(as of a debt).

-

The Greek god of silence.

R

RAMIFY

(RAM-i-fy)

transitive, intransitive verb:

To divide into branches.

-

Vigorous sexual intercourse.

RAPPORTEUR

(ra-por-TER) noun:

A person who gives reports

(as at a meeting of a

learned society).

-

An old-school rap fan.

REBUFF

(rih-BUFF) verb:

To reject or criticize sharply.

-

To get undressed.

REECHY

(REE-chee) adjective:
Moky, dirty, or rancid.

-

Reaching across someone
without saying, "Excuse me."

REMORA

(REM-er-uh) noun:

An obstacle, hindrance,

or obstruction.

-

A suburb of Gomorrah.

RESILE

(rih-ZYLE) verb:

Recoil, retract; especially to

return to a prior position.

-

Residing on an island.

RETRODICTION

(ret-roh-DIK-shuhn) verb:
Using present information
to make an assertion
about the past.

-

Old slang.

REVENANT

(rev-uh-nt) noun:
One who returns after death
(as a ghost) or
after a long absence.

-

A non rent-paying tenant.

RUTILANT

(ROOT-l-uhnt) adjective:
Glowing or glittering with
ruddy or golden light.

-

Rude but brilliant.

S

SAGACITY

(suh-GAS-i-tee) noun:

Keen judgment or wisdom.

-

Where wise people live.

SANSCULOTTE

(sanz-koo-LAHT) noun:

A radical or violent

extremist in politics.

-

A picnic without Kool Aid.

SARDANAPALIAN

(sahr-dn-uh-PEYL-yuhn)

adjective:

Excessively luxurious.

-

Unadorned sandals;

basic flip flops.

SATYR

(SAY-tuhr, SAT-uhr) noun:

A lecherous man.

-

A special Jewish feast.

SCARAMOUCH

(SKAIR-uh-moosh) noun:

A cowardly buffoon.

-

How to get your

money back from a deadbeat.

SCHLOCKMEISTER

(SHLOK-my-stuhr) noun:

One who deals in

inferior goods.

-

Day manager at a strip club.

SCOTOPHOBIA

(sko-tuh-FOH-bee-uh) noun:

Fear of the dark.

-

Fear of Scott Bakula.

SCUPPER

(SKUP-uhr) noun, transitive
verb:
To prevent from succeeding.

-

Digging the last bit of ice cream
out of the bottom of the
container.

SELCOUTH

(SEL-kooth) adjective:

Strange; uncommon.

-

What charm schools do.

SEQUACIOUS

(sih-KWAY-shus) adjective:

Intellectually servile.

-

A sexy tree.

SERIOCOMIC

(seer-ee-oh-KAH-mik)
adjective:
Having a mixture of the
serious and the comic.

-

A political comedian.

SHIV

(shiv) noun:

A knife, especially a
switchblade.

-

An abbreviated period
of mourning.

SIBILANT

(SIB-uh-luhnt) adjective:

Hissing.

-

A combative sibling.

SKIRR

(skur) verb:

To go rapidly; fly; scurry.

-

A short skirt.

SLIMSY

(SLIM-zee) adjective:

Flimsy; frail.

-

1. Slim Shady's Fremen name.

2. An upper case, sans serif "z."

SMASHMOUTH

(SMASH-mouth) adjective:
Characterized by brute
force without finesse.

-

An awkward first kiss.

SOLECISM

(SOL-uh-siz-uhm) noun:
A breach of good
manners or etiquette.

-

Foot amputation.

SPLEENFUL

(SPLEEN-fuhl) adjective:
Ill-humored; irritable or
peevish; spiteful; splenetic.

-

An overworked spleen.

SPLENDIFEROUS

(splen-DIF-er-uhs) adjective:
Magnificent; fine.

-

Thinking Splenda
tastes better than sugar.

SPOONERISM

(SPOO-nuh-riz-um) noun:
The transposition of (usually)
the initial sounds of words
producing a humorous result.

-

Followers of Uri Geller.

STEM-WINDER

(STEM-wyne-der) noun:

A stem-winding watch.

-

A frontal wedgie.

SUASION

(SWAY-zhuhn) noun:
The act of urging; persuasion.

-

Telling someone not
to put baby in the corner.

SUBSTRATE

(SUHB-streyt) noun:
Something that is spread
or laid under something else.

-

Living below the poverty line.

SUDORIFIC

(soo-duh-RIF-ik) adjective:
Causing sweat.

-

Not as great as you
thought it would be.

SYLPH

(SILF) noun:

A slender graceful
woman or girl.

-

A syphilitic elf.

T

TAWPIE

(TAW-pee) noun:

A foolish or thoughtless
young person.

-

Slightly brown in color.

TELLURIAN

(te-LOOR-ee-uhn) adjective,

noun:

An inhabitant of the earth.

-

A DeLorean salesperson.

TEMPESTUOUS

(tem-PESS-chuh-wus) adjective:
Of, relating to, or resembling a
tempest; turbulent, stormy.

-

An angry Wookie.

TENABLE

(TEN-uh-buhl) adjective:
Capable of being held
or defended.

-

A child's ability to
count to 10.

TETRALOGY

(teh-TRAH-luh-jee) noun:
A series of four connected
literary, artistic,
or musical works.

-

The study of *Tetris.*

TITUBANT

(TICH-oo-buhnt) noun:
A disturbance of body
equilibrium in standing or
walking, resulting in an
uncertain gait and trembling.

-

Perky breasts.

TOME

(TOHM) noun:
A volume forming part
of a larger work.

-

How Dan Quayle
spells "Tom."

TOPLOFTY

(TAHP-lawf-tee) adjective:

Very superior in air or attitude.

-

The view from the top bunk.

TORRID

(TOR-id) adjective:
Parched with heat,
especially of the sun; hot.

-

When Tori Spelling is
in a bad mood.

TRAJECT

(truh-JEKT) verb:
To transport, transmit,
or transpose.

-

When something tragic
happens in the projects.

TUB-THUMPER

(TUB-thump-er) noun:
A vociferous supporter
(as of a cause).

The song that made
Chumbawamba
a one-hit wonder.

U

UNABASHED

(un-uh-BASHT) adjective:

Not disconcerted; undisguised.

-

Getting uninvited

from a big party.

UNAVAILING

(uhn-uh-VEY-ling) adjective:
Futile.

-

Sending avails to a local
comedy club that
never uses you.

UNBOLTED

(un-BOHL-tud) adjective:

Not sifted.

-

Not wearing a girdle.

UNCANNY

(un-KAN-ee) adjective:

Eerie, mysterious.

-

Drinking 7 Up from a glass.

UNDULATE

(UN-juh-layt) verb:

To fluctuate.

-

Refusing to pay a
bill until its overdue.

UNFETTERED

(un-FET-erd) adjective:

Free, unrestrained.

-

When you go to someone's
house and they don't offer you
food or drink.

UNWIELDY

(un-WEEL-dee) adjective:

Cumbersome.

-

A car tire blow out.

UTILE

(YOO-til) adjective:

Useful.

-

Personally preparing
soil to grow crops.

V

VADE MECUM

(vay-dee-MEE-kum) noun:

A book for ready

reference; manual.

-

Darth Vader's

Latin (stripper) name.

VALIDATE

(VAL-uh-dayt) verb:

To make legally valid; ratify.

-

Going on a date with a valley
girl.

VALOROUS

(VAL-uh-russ) adjective:
Possessing or acting
with bravery or boldness.

-

The male form of Valerie.

VAMP

(vamp) verb:

To patch up; repair.

-

A character who is required

to spend 50% of their

on-screen time naked.

VARLET

(VAHR-lit) noun:

A knavish person; rascal.

-

A beautiful, young

Viking film star.

VENTOSE

(VEN-tohs) adjective:

Given to empty talk; windy.

-

Open-toed shoes.

VERSICOLOR

(VUR-si-kuhl-er) adjective:
Changeable in color.

-

African American poetry.

VIAND

(VYE-und) noun:

An item of food.

-

When a man realizes that
romance requires more than
Viagra.

VIGORISH

(VIG-er-ish) noun:

Interest paid to a moneylender,

especially a usurer.

-

A strong craving for licorice.

VILIPEND

(vil-UH-pend) verb:
To regard or treat as of
little value or account.

-

To add an extension
onto the villa.

VOLANT

(VOH-lunt) adjective:
Having the wings extended
as if in flight —
used of a heraldic bird.

-

A violent Vulcan.
(See Romulan.)

VOLUME MAMMOSE

(VOL-yoom MAM-ohs) adjective:

Having large breasts.

-

A moose with many offspring.

VOTARY

(VOH-tuh-ree) noun:

One who is devoted, given,

or addicted to some particular

pursuit, subject, study,

or way of life.

-

Voting in every election.

W

WELKIN

(WEL-kin) noun:
The vault of the sky; heaven.

-

Having a healthy family.

WELTSCHMERZ

(VELT-shmairts) noun:

Often capitalized: mental
depression or apathy caused by
comparison of the actual state
of the world with an ideal state.

-

When Ethel hit Fred.

WETWARE

(WET-wair) noun:

The human brain.

-

A bathing suit.

WIDDERSHINS

(WID-er-shinz) adverb:
In a left-handed, wrong, or
contrary direction;
counterclockwise.

-

The gateway to cankles.

341

WILLOWWACKS

(WIL-oh-waks) noun:

A wooded, uninhabited area.

-

What Willow on

Buffy the Vampire Slayer

does when she's bored.

WINSOME

(WIN-sum) adjective:
Generally pleasing and
engaging often because of a
childlike charm and innocence.

-

What occasionally happens
in Las Vegas.

WUNDERKIND

(VOON-duhr-kind) noun:
A child prodigy.

When you don't know why
someone has done
something nice for you.

X

XENOPHILIA

(zen-uh-FIL-ee-uh) noun:

An attraction to foreign

peoples, cultures, or customs.

-

Love of *Xena: Warrior Princess.*

X-RAY

(eks-ray) noun:

A communications code word

for the letter "x."

-

Jamie Foxx.

Y

YEOMAN

(YOH-mun) noun:
An officer in the U.S. Navy
who works as a clerk.

-

A yes man.

Z

ZEBULON

(zeb-yuh-lon, -luh n) noun:

A male given name.

-

The hillbilly home world.

ABOUT THE AUTHOR

If you have cable or more than 2G-access to the Internet you may have seen stand-up comedian Leighann Lord on ABC's *The View,* Comedy Central, Lifetime, and HBO. She has performed for audiences around the world at colleges, comedy clubs, theaters, and war zones including Afghanistan, Iraq, and TGI Friday's (A good margarita is worth fighting for). Leighann earned her Bachelor of Arts in Journalism and Creative Writing from Baruch College, City University of New York. While she owes no student loans, she is one of Visa's long-time indentured servants. Leighann is a New York City native, a queen from Queens, and a would-be member of the House of Ravenclaw.

www.VeryFunnyLady.com